What's Up with your PumpKin?

Keys and Steps to Reaching Your Dreams

By John L. Dammarell

What's Up
with your
Pumpkin?

Keys and Steps to Reaching Your Dreams

John L. Dammarell

WESTBOW
PRESS®
A DIVISION OF THOMAS NELSON
& ZONDERVAN

WestBow Press books may be ordered through booksellers or by contacting:

WestBow Press
A Division of Thomas Nelson & Zondervan
1663 Liberty Drive
Bloomington, IN 47403
www.westbowpress.com
1 (866) 928-1240

ISBN: 978-1-9736-2021-1 (sc)
ISBN: 978-1-9736-2023-5 (hc)
ISBN: 978-1-9736-2022-8 (e)

Library of Congress Control Number: 2018902107

Print information available on the last page.

WestBow Press rev. date: 3/16/2018

FOREWORD

John's story is a profoundly powerful example of a man with a dream put to action. He is not a daydreamer, but a man with a big dream empowered by great steps of faith. I have the privilege of watching John's dream come to life in the stories of the hundreds of lives his work is touching. This book will not only inspire you to dream big, but to act on that dream. Active dreamers like John change the world for the better. I'm honored to not only watch this dream unfold, but to be a friend of the dreamer.

~ HR Huntsman, Executive Coach and author of *Reason to Believe* (Huntsman Publishing, 2012)

Praise for

What's Up with Your Pumpkin?

This is a lighthearted allegory involving the life span of a pumpkin from seed to table. John has delightfully depicted, in detail, the very heart of the birth (seed) and germination (watering and feeding) and consumption of the fruit (realization of your dream). *What's Up With Your Pumpkin?* is easy to read, inspiring, and motivational!

~ Jennifer Adkisson, Mrs. Washington 2007, Cheney, WA

Timeless profound lessons framed in a simple short story told by a man of God that epitomizes the purpose Jesus has for every one of us! Really well done, John! Thank you for your story telling and, more importantly, thank you for being the example to all of us of HIS love and grace!

~ Curt Altig, CEO, Builders Capital, Seattle, WA

Maybe one of the best books I have ever had the opportunity to read. This is spot on in all aspects of: Vision! Faith! Persistence! Takes me from Old Testament to New with all of King's Word to back! John lives this! Inspires me! Love this! Huge! Awesome! Amen! So good!!!

~ Roger Blier, CEO & Co-Founder, Passport Unlimited, Kirkland, WA

Anyone who has met John Dammarell—and others who haven't—will enjoy looking through this window into his soul. As they read, they will suspect that he has somehow peered into their souls as well and take counsel from what he has seen.

~ Dr. Joseph Castleberry, President, Northwest University, and author of *Your Deepest Dream* (Navpress, 2012)

This book will reinvigorate your passion for dreaming and living big. It's a hands-on guide to help you live your dreams, not for yourself, but to bring significance to others in accordance with God's plan. God has truly blessed me by bringing John into my life. Awesome work, buddy!

~ Michael S. Clark, Attorney-at-Law, The Law Offices of Krupa & Clark, Tacoma, WA

John is a man of action. What you are going to read is powerful, but the man is even more significant. If more people did what John has done, our communities would be ablaze for Jesus. Read these words, study these words, and live these words.

~ Dean G. Curry, Senior Pastor, Life Center, Tacoma, WA

Pastor John walks his readers through the beautiful hope found in the amazing promises of a very faithful God. Dreams, like pumpkin seeds, flourish when surrendered and entrusted into the hands of the Creator of all things. Thank you, John. You are an example to all of us!!!

~ Steve Esau, VP of Sales & Co-Founder, Passport Unlimited, Kirkland, WA

John's book will leave you inspired and riveted to the core to fulfill the dreams of God for your life. John's life is one of destiny that has possessed the rebounding, unrelenting power of God through many seasons. It is my prayer you'd catch that same power as you read his story and hear the heart of God for the dreams *He* has put in your heart!

~ Jude Fouquier, Senior Pastor, The City Church, Ventura, CA

Like many of our favorite rock stars in the Bible, John could be, and should be one of them. His belief and expectation for the goodness God has planned in our life is remarkable, even through the challenges he's endured. This is an encouraging and powerful read that will bless you!

~ Mike Friedrich, AdvoCare Independent Distributor, Woodinville, WA

Dreams, like pumpkin seeds, go through seasons, storms and delays. John has likened fulfillment of a dream to the growth of a pumpkin seed maturing to a full plant. He has masterfully assembled profound lessons, all from scripture, that will help you kick-start and fulfill your dream. These lessons will help you overcome the procrastinations and failures of your past. John is a living example of these principles. By the power of God, he lives what he writes. Thank you, John.

~ Ron Harris, President, Valley Harvest Products, Tukwila, WA

Pastor John Dammarell's name really should be "Johnny Pumpkin Seed." He has helped nourish the seeds of dreams in countless lives, especially mine. This book will take you on an amazing journey toward growing your own God-inspired pumpkins, one seed at a time.

~ Doug Myers, Principal & General Partner, Edward Jones, Des Moines, WA

John Dammarell gives a compilation of some of the best success principles for life in a short and compelling story. Take the best five books on success and consolidate them into one usable and potent story and you have *What's Up With Your Pumpkin?*

~ Jeff Rogers, Chairman & CEO, OneAccord, Bellevue, WA

Dreams are a dime a dozen unfortunately. What we are really looking for are new enlightening realities that are the result of dreams that never died, or as John has so aptly put it, "never were planted." John Dammarell is a dreamer, who has lived exactly what he has written, and has put together a wise plan for making *your* dreams a reality. It's time for us to wake up, plant those hopeful realities in the fresh soil of now and work to see our pumpkins, (*ahem*) dreams, come true.

~ Royce Wilson, Senior Pastor, StoryChurch, Bothell, WA

ACKNOWLEDGEMENTS

My good friend, Doug Myers, was instrumental in challenging business leaders to grow a pumpkin and likened that to growing our dreams. We were to come back in a few months and tell the story of our journey. I took the challenge and I have Doug to thank for inspiring me to write this book.

My wife, Karilyn Dammarell, spent countless hours editing and listening to me read portions of the book. I am so grateful for the treasure she is in my life. Karilyn is my best friend, my lover, my prayer partner, my inspiration.

My children, Howard, Christie, David and Charlie and my stepchildren, Jennifer and Theo listened when I would ask, "Can you listen to what I just wrote?"

Geoff Pope, Editor Extraordinaire and friend, edited and edited and edited my book. Brendon Bannon, Illustrator, listened to me and made those pumpkins come to life.

My good friends, Ron Harris and Curt Altig, spent hours listening to me run ideas past them.

And, I am forever grateful to Debra Bartell, our good friend, for her prayers and hours of encouragement AND for underwriting the publishing of this book.

CONTENTS

Acknowledgements.. xvii

Introduction xxi

Chapter 1   The Seed of Your Dream 1

Chapter 2   Knowing the What and
            Why of Your Dream...13

Chapter 3   Preparation: The Key to Realizing the
            Success of Your Dream.......................................21

Chapter 4   Believe Your Dream 43

Chapter 5   Passion for Your Dream.....................................57

Chapter 6   The Significance of Your Dream 63

A Dialogue on Parting Thoughts...67

            Session 1: Chapter 1.. 68

            Session 2: Chapter 2 69

            Sessions 3 & 4: Chapter 3 70

            Session 5: Chapters 4 & 5 73

            Session 6: Chapter 6 75

INTRODUCTION

Some of you have gone through tough times and had unfair things happen in your life. Perhaps life hasn't turned out the way you had hoped it would. You could easily be discouraged and give up on your dreams. I know; I've been there. I have gone through so much stuff that I thought all my dreams and aspirations in life were over. Yet, in my darkest of moments, God reminded me of a young man in the Bible whose name was Joseph. If Joseph were to speak to us today, he would say, "Don't get discouraged. Don't give up on your dream. I had a dream, and I knew God's hand was upon me even though my brothers were against me. For many years it seemed like there was no possible way my dream would be realized, yet I didn't give up. One day, God turned it all around and brought it to pass."

I am telling you this to encourage you to not give up on what's in your heart. Circumstances may not have gone the way you had hoped. People may have wounded you; but if you keep believing, even though it's hard, the same God who gave you the seed of your dream will bring it to pass.

So what's up with your dreams? What's your story? God put that dream seed in your heart, yet you have been reluctant to plant it. Maybe you've had one of those daring dreams where you believed you would one day parachute out of an airplane, free falling thousands of feet before your parachute opens and glides you gently to the ground. Maybe it's a book you're always going to write, a preparedness program you are going to do, an invention you are going to create, an exercise program you are going to start, or a business you dreamed you would start.

Jon, my good friend and business owner, had a dream. He had been homeless on the streets of Seattle for nine years when one day God took hold of his life and changed him. He filled Jon with hope, planting a dream seed in his heart to start a cleaning business. Jon persevered with newfound faith. He worked diligently. He prayed as if it all depended on God, and his dream was eventually realized. Today Jon runs a very successful business, making a significant impact on the community. Life is full of dreams and ideas.

It's with this that I want to share with you the story of my journey. It's an amazing journey—a journey fictitious in nature that will take you into an imaginary world. Perhaps you can remember when you were a child and what you were going to be when you grew up: a fireman or a policeman or an entrepreneur who made lots of money as an owner of a large company. Or maybe you dreamed you were a Princess and someday Prince Charming would ride into your life, sweep you off your feet, and you would live happily ever after. Perhaps your imaginary world was filled with people, lots of people; and in your dream, all these people worked for you because you owned the business and you were going to make lots of money.

As you travel with me on my journey, I ask you to ask yourself this question: "What's up with your dream?" You see, my dream started when one of my board members was sharing on growing your business. He likened it to a farmer who has to go out and plant his seed to receive a harvest. He encouraged us to plant our dreams; and with those dreams, to walk in significance. To illustrate his point, he gave us all pumpkin seeds, challenging us to grow a pumpkin and then to come back to share our journey. I bought into the challenge. I grew a pumpkin and a very large pumpkin at that. It was a simple dream but very meaningful, one that would have lasting effects on my life. Now you might be thinking, "What in the world is there about growing a pumpkin that can affect my life? Is this just another bedtime story I can read to my children or grandchildren or, is it really something that goes much deeper than that?" Well, I'll leave it up to you at this point. However, you just might find that those ideas and those dreams you have had may actually become a reality. They just might happen. SO GET READY.

1

THE SEED OF YOUR DREAM

My story begins with a seed. However, this is not just some ordinary seed. This is a seed designed to grow a giant pumpkin. Now we all know when you plant a pumpkin seed, you do it with the thought that you're going to grow a pumpkin. However, my dream was that my seed would grow into the biggest pumpkin anyone had ever seen. As long as the seeds stayed in the little envelope, there would be no pumpkin. I had to make a decision to plant my pumpkin seeds.

I asked myself, do I really want to grow a pumpkin? I mean, this is really kind of ridiculous.

There must be a time commitment involved. I have started so many things in the past and never finished them. Besides, I have never grown a pumpkin before. To do this I would be journeying into unchartered waters. Then my mind raced back to the time when I was a child. My mother and father always planted a garden, and I remember being so fascinated with the lushness of it. They grew the very best carrots and peas. Those peas were yummy, so yummy that I would eat them right off the vine. My mother would catch me and say, "Johnny, don't eat them all or we won't have any for dinner." Well, one day I said to my mom, "Mother, may I plant my own garden?" So she gave me a little spot, and I planted the seeds for my garden. But something awful happened. Nothing grew! Now I thought to myself, *"Would the same thing happen?* Would my pumpkin seeds fail to grow? Do I really want to make the sacrifices it's going to take to grow my pumpkin?" We remember so much about our past failures, fears, pain of rejection, and the bitterness of loss. *Will I have the time to do this? On top of it all, I lack experience.* But guess what? I decided to take a chance and be a risk-taker. I was not going to let my fears and past failures dictate my present and my future. I was going to grow a pumpkin.

The journey began as I asked myself some important questions. *Why am I growing this pumpkin, and what do I hope to achieve?* The *Why* and *What* proved essential in helping me to stay on track and not lose my way on the journey toward growing my pumpkin. This meant I was going to need to read the directions. *Directions? No, please, not directions!* You don't understand or maybe you do. This is hard for me. I don't like to read directions.

Then I thought to myself, *This is what I will do. I will take a shortcut and read just part of the directions.* It said to plant the seed one inch beneath the surface of the soil, so I did. What I failed to do was read where it said to use *fresh* and *fertile* soil. At that moment, I had no idea that my shortcut and my impatience would be the beginning of what I never would have anticipated.

At the time we lived in a townhome and the only flowers we could grow were grown in pots. Therefore, I knew I was going to have to grow my pumpkin in a pot. So I thought to myself, *You can do this. That's right, you just have to believe you can. Just have a passion for what you are doing.* So I planted my pumpkin seed and woke up every day with anticipation, expecting soon that I would see the pumpkin plant poking through the soil. I was so excited when I came home from work that I would go immediately to my pumpkin pot and poke my finger around where I had planted the seeds. You would have thought that I had just won a million dollar prize when I yelled with excitement, "My pumpkin seed is growing! My pumpkin seed is growing!" However, it wasn't very many days later when something terrible happened...something I never anticipated. My pumpkin looked like it was dying! *Why was this happening to me? What went wrong? I thought I was doing everything right. I read the directions; well, part of them.* So I said, "I know what I need to do. I need to call my farmer friends because they will know how to grow pumpkins."

"Hello, is this Carolyn?...Listen I have a problem. I planted some pumpkin seeds in a pot, and they started to grow but died. What did I do wrong? Can you help me?" She told me that I needed to get rid of that old rotten soil in the pot; to purchase some really good rich, fertile soil; and to control the watering. So I went to the nursery and bought the very best potting soil I could find and planted new seeds. Carolyn suggested I also go on the internet and read what I could find on *growing* pumpkins. As I did, I began to nourish my dream of growing pumpkins. I decided I wanted to become the best pumpkin grower possible, and my excitement grew exponentially about the process.

I awakened each day with a passion for my goal. I could hardly wait until my pumpkin seed began to push through the soil. I just knew with all the mentorship and learning, this time I was not going to fail. It was with heightened passion and anticipation that I checked my pumpkin seed each morning before I went to work and again at night when I arrived home from work. I remembered my pumpkin mentors had told me that I needed to carefully watch over my pumpkin plant every day. They warned me of all kinds of little varmints that would try to suck the life out of my plants. As my pumpkin started to grow, I was on high alert, watching out for the "pumpkin gang" known to smash pumpkins as they grew.

Concerned as I was, I spoke with my neighbor and asked him if he would be willing to help guard my pumpkin. I even swore him in as the head of the Pumpkin Guard Patrol. Now my pumpkin plant was growing fast! Then one day it happened. I started to see a real pumpkin growing on my plant. I thought, "Wow! I finally have my pumpkin." It wasn't long and then...pow!! The unexpected happened! My pumpkin was beginning to shrivel up! Every day it got smaller and uglier. Then I noticed about two feet farther down the vine toward the end, *another* pumpkin was growing.

I jumped on the phone and called my pumpkin mentors who told me to cut the sick pumpkin from the vine because it was sucking all the energy from the little pumpkin at the end. What?! You've got to be kidding...cut off my pumpkin! I can't do it. I have spent so much time and energy in growing this pumpkin. I have invested so much into it. But following the advice of my mentor, I knew what I had to do. SNIP. SNIP. And...almost as if a small miracle had taken place, the little pumpkin began to grow and grow. Each day as I arrived home from work, I would look at my pumpkin. The day finally arrived when I called some of my younger grandchildren to come over to help Grandpa cut his pumpkin. "Grandpa, I love your pumpkin. It's big and so beautiful." Success had come at last, but there is more to this story. My neighbor, who had been watching me grow my pumpkin and whom I had enlisted to be head of the Pumpkin Guard Patrol, saw my pumpkin near our outside door. He said to me, "I've been watching you grow your pumpkin and have even helped you at times, so I was wondering if next year we could grow pumpkins together? You can show me how, and we can see who can grow the BIGGEST PUMPKIN.

The realization of all our dreams, as it did with the growing of my pumpkin, really starts with a seed, much like an idea, or a thought. How many innovative, creative ideas have you had in the course of your years, only to find yourself saying, "I should have done something with that idea. Why, I just read the other day, the very idea I had twenty years ago is now on some of our newest cars. *"What's with that? I should have done this. I should have done that. What if I had not been such a procrastinator?"* How characteristic this is of many of us. I'm thinking of all the conversations I have had with friends; all their "if-onlys," "what-ifs," and "I should-haves," but they never or rarely did anything with their dreams. A friend of mine recently shared with me how he had been a procrastinator most of his life but decided he was going to go ahead and write a book he had talked about doing for years. He was convinced that God had planted the seed in his heart, and finally he needed to do something with it.

It's story after story: businesses that were going to be started, books that were going to be written, inventions that could have become a reality, and programs that were going to be created; yet those seeds still remain in an envelope, placed on a shelf. Oh, we bring it down now and then and kind of toss it around. We even go so far as to tell others, "Someday I'm going to do this." Yet for whatever reason, we stick it back on the shelf where it waits and waits to be planted.

2

KNOWING THE WHAT AND WHY OF YOUR DREAM

In the process of beginning my journey to fulfilling my dream, I had to ask myself the hard questions about growing my pumpkin. Why am I growing this pumpkin and what do I hope to achieve by it? Understanding your *why* keeps you motivated and excited about what you are doing. Without an understanding of your *why* and your *what*, you will have a very difficult time getting through the struggles and challenges you will face. You will become easily discouraged and ready to throw in the towel. As you become distracted, you will be tempted to take shortcuts that, at the moment, might seem very enticing, but in the long run are dead-end streets.

Curt, CEO of a business in Seattle, says, "The *why* is the beacon that keeps you focused when everything seems so challenging and confusing." Knowing your *why* allows clients and potential clients to discern an authenticity and joy in you and in what you do. When your "What" and "Why" go beyond yourself, that's when you really begin to make an impact. How do we define the "Why" that goes beyond ourselves? We could contrast it with the typical understanding of the "Why," which is much like the corporate ladder that, for instance, can be very self-oriented, self-fulfilling, and even self-serving. When you are concerned about climbing the corporate ladder, your whole *why* becomes focused on using and manipulating people, which even begins to compromise your values. You may do whatever it takes and whatever it costs to get to the top of the ladder—gaining position, power, and prestige. This can be very self-focused. However, on the other hand, you have the *Jesus* "Why." Here Jesus is the prime example when He said, "I come not to be served but to serve and give my life as a ransom for many." This "Why" is based on three building blocks: Service, Generosity, and Relationship. The Jesus "Why" cuts at the very core of *self*-focus converting it to *other*-focus.

Let's say your dream is to start a business. There are three reasons why clarifying your Jesus "Why" is so important:

1. It gives you a greater reason to get up in the morning. Your business/life is focused on serving, giving, and making a difference in your community.

15

2. It gives you a greater passion for what you do. Passion is what drives you through challenges because you know at the end of the day your business is about others—not just yourself.

3. It helps you to determine the important from the urgent. Urgent is the distractions, such as the-grass-is-greener-on-the-other-side *or* get-rich-quick schemes.

A friend of ours, Laurie, further gives five reasons why clarifying your "Why" is so important:

1. Sharing your "Why" with others builds relationships.

2. It gives clients confidence in you and your work.

3. You will naturally lead, because people want to follow someone who knows where they are going and are passionate about what they do.

4. You will do your work with more enthusiasm, joy, and passion.

5. It sets you apart from your competition.

This principle, the Jesus "Why," should apply to all of our dreams, whether it's starting a business, writing a book, climbing a mountain, etc. Let's say for example, that it's your desire to lose fifty pounds. Now you'll hear this from almost every trainer: *Do it for yourself.* However, with the Jesus "Why," it's about being *other*-focused. The primary reason you're doing this would be: I don't want to leave my wife a young widow nor deny the opportunity of mentorship to my grandchildren, etc. See how that works? *Other* focus. Much like what I chose to do with my pumpkin. The next year I would show my neighbor how to grow pumpkins, and we would do it together.

Let me further illustrate how this Jesus "Why"

plays out. I was out running one day and I asked myself why I was doing this with all the aches and pain I had. I could just sleep in a little longer and besides, it's cold outside. There must be a greater motivation. I recalled how I share with others how important it is to ask this question: "How does what I'm doing have a significant value to it?" In other words, how will this discipline make a difference in others? So I decided I would call it "Running for Significance." Therefore, I would look for sponsors to sponsor me for every mile that I would run over the next forty days, then donate that money to a project of one of Liberty Road Foundation's non-profit partners. Through this process you would not believe how much more value and importance this brought to my running. My motivation, the very thing that gets me up earlier and enables me to look beyond the excuses has become: *I am running for others.*

Now my running has a greater significant value to it. Or let's consider again the person who wants to lose fifty pounds. He or she could find sponsors for every pound they lose over the next ninety days and then give that money to their favorite charity. Again, asking the question, *How does what I am doing have a significant value to it?* Or perhaps you're not really into raising money, but you still want to help others. It may be mowing a lawn for the neighbor, helping a widow pick up her groceries, or reading stories to elderly people at an assisted living home.

3

PREPARATION: THE KEY TO REALIZING THE SUCCESS OF YOUR DREAM

Well, John, isn't the success of our dreams really dependent on how well we prepare? Ecclesiastes 5:3a says, *"For the dream comes through much effort"* *(NASB).* This verse really describes why a lot of people give up on their dreams before they ever get started. What separates the seed of the dream from the germination of the dream is a lot of work, which entails preparation—my pumpkin plant failed simply because I failed to make proper preparations.

So often, when people find out it will take effort,

or be costly and uncomfortable to complete the preparation for the birth of their dream, they shelve the idea. They make the excuse, "It probably wasn't God's will after all." Football coach Vince Lombardi put it well: "The will to win is not nearly so important as the will to prepare to win." Most people have the will to win. Most people enjoy winning and all that comes with it. The people that are willing to put in the hard work and the time required to prepare to win are far more rare. Great performers have that rare will to prepare.

It was John Wooden, the former UCLA basketball coach who said, "If you don't have time to do it right, when will you have time to do it over?" It has been said that he would spend hours upon hours going over details. And it was John Maxwell who said, "We cannot become what we need to be by remaining what we are." In other words, practice,

practice, practice. God has given us example after example in nature on how important preparation is. For instance, he speaks of the ant that needs no leader, no prodding from anyone. He simply goes out and prepares his food in the summer and gathers his food at harvest so that he is prepared for the long winters. There are three basic keys in the preparation process.

1st Key – Know Well the Directions for Your Dream

Directions. What is this about? One of my greatest pet peeves in my life is having to read directions and especially having to ask for them. You know what that's like. You have been invited to someone's house for dinner where you've never been; and instead of consulting the direction finder, you launch off on your own. You finally give up when you're an hour late and call for directions. Then, you come to the intelligent conclusion that you should have gotten directions before you started out. Many should-haves could have been avoided if you had asked for or read the directions.

Let's say you want to start a business. After you have determined the "Why" and the "What" of your business, it becomes necessary that you surround yourself with wise and knowledgeable people who will instruct you with the "how to's" of your business. Proverbs 3:13 *"Happy is the man who finds wisdom, and the man who gains understanding" (NKJV)*. It's been said that we need to be a lifelong learner in order to be successful in what we do. And Proverbs 3:5—6 tells us to *"Trust in the Lord with all your heart, and lean not on your own understanding; in all your ways acknowledge Him, and He shall direct your path" (NKJV)*. It is important that we acknowledge God's Word is filled with the directions we need for the fulfillment of our dreams, and in particular, the dream to start a business. Here are just a few scriptures that will act as action steps that, when adhered to, will have a huge impact on the success of your dreams.

Action Step #1: Always Be Open To What God Wants

"Behold I will do something new, now it will spring forth; will you not be aware of it? I will even make a roadway in the wilderness, rivers in the desert" (Isaiah 43:19, *NASB)*. Sometimes your business will need to move as the market pulls in a different direction. You might need to reinvent your business. You should not fear. God will always have your back.

Let's look at another example. It's your dream to start an exercise program. You've been running a certain way for months, and it seems that you have just hit a wall. You feel like you're going nowhere. This happened to me until a friend came along and lined out a whole new running plan, much different than what I was doing. You would not believe the results. This raises a question: Are you prepared that God just might want to reinvent your dream?

Action Step #2: Pray, Pray, Pray

"Be anxious for nothing, but in everything by prayer and supplication with thanksgiving let your requests be made known to God" (Phil. 4:6, *NASB*). One of the best things you can do for the success of your dream is to pray for it. Be specific and always pray your request with faith and expectation. Ephesians 3:20—21 tells us, *"Now to Him who is able to do far more abundantly beyond all that we ask or think, according to the power that works within us, to Him be the glory in the church and in Christ Jesus to all generations forever and ever. Amen"*

(NASB). God's plan for that dream you have may very well far exceed your thoughts and your ideas. We have a God with the wildest imagination. He just might very well surprise you!

Action Step #3: Focus On the Positive

"For as he thinks in his heart, so is he" (Proverbs 23:7a, *NKJV*). Our thoughts can become the biggest obstacles and distractions in the success of our dreams. What are those influencers that you allow your mind to focus on in the course of a day's time? It's often been said that it takes many positive thoughts to counteract one negative thought. Check out what you read, what you listen to, and the people who surround you. It's all about choice. It's up to you to use discretion and discernment in choosing the influencers you will allow to speak into your life. Your ability to think positively, to see the glass

half-full not half-empty, and to learn from your experiences and shake off your mistakes, will be a huge help in the right direction.

"Overwhelming Truth: Perspective is everything. How can we not keep our chin up and live with gratitude when we know our future of FOREVER with Christ? It always blows my mind: FOREVER. Think about that. Pain is temporary. Setbacks affect us greatly because we are human and we can get shortsighted oftentimes. However, when we are reminded of the overwhelming truth that we are saved by the grace of God and that is truly all that matters, then it is hard to stay negative or in a diminished state. The life of each and every one of our Bible heroes can give us hope. Every single one of them got negative and suffered great turmoil. However, they rose above it as they had a higher and deeper purpose of living for the Glory of God! Let that thought prop your chin up today and Praise the Lord!!"

~ Ron Alford, Southwestern Consulting, Kent, Washington

Action Step #4: Relax In God's Timing

Finally, when dealing with establishing direction for your dreams, you will need to remember it's all about timing. *"But these things I plan won't happen right away. Slowly, steadily, surely, the time approaches when the vision will be fulfilled. If it seems slow, do not despair, for these things will surely come to pass. Just be patient! They will not be overdue a single day!"* (Habakkuk 2:3, *TLB*). His time is not always our time. There may be a time in that business you are starting, that book you are writing, or that exercise program you just started, that you just get bogged down. It doesn't seem like it's going anywhere. It's like you have crashed into a wall. Or perhaps you thought it was going one way and it's going another. Those are the times you need to put your trust in God the most, being aware that it's all about His timing. Philippians 2:13 says, *"For it is God who is at work in you, both to will and to work for His good pleasure" (NASB)*. We can trust the Lord, knowing that He is our empowerer. To empower someone is to give means, authority, or power to do what you have directed them to accomplish. He not only supplies us with all that we need according to His sufficient grace, but He effects the changes in, through, and with us for His good pleasure.

Action Step #5: Choose Carefully Those Influencers In Your Life

"Where there is no guidance the people fall, but in abundance of counselors there is victory" (Proverbs 11:14,

NASB). Just as I needed my farmer friends as mentors to succeed in growing my pumpkin, you need mentors with your dream. Officer John, one of our business leaders, shared this: "If I involve my mentor, it is easier to stay on target because he will hold me accountable." Mentorship, as defined by Wikipedia, "is a relationship in which a more experienced or more knowledgeable person helps to guide a less experienced or less knowledgeable person." What are some thoughts on choosing your mentors?

1. More than one mentor is better. The Scripture says, *"…in abundance of counselors there is victory"* (Proverbs 11:14, *NASB*).

2. Make a list of those who are both knowledgeable and full of wisdom that you would want on your list.

3. Pray over the list, specifically asking God to show you whom to ask. *"The mind of man plans*

his way, but the Lord directs his steps" (Proverbs 16:9, *NASB*).

4. A mentor is a powerful role model. Therefore, look for someone of great character who is an example of what he or she says.

5. Look for mentors who are creative, honest, empathetic, authentic, and faith builders.

6. Be forever grateful for the mentorship received so that your mentors are not taken for granted.

2nd Key – Concern Yourself with Excellence

"You see a man skilled in his work? He will stand before kings; he will not stand before obscure men" (Proverbs 22:29, *NASB*). It has often been said that God is in the promotion business. Your part is to become everything you can with the skills and talents you have been given, paying attention to detail, getting

proper training, acquiring mentorship, and working hard. God will take care of the winning. We simply prepare to win with all the excellence we have and leave the success up to Him.

John Maxwell says, "Excellence is the gap between average and exceptional." He further says, "It's the ability to exceed expectations and consistently deliver superior quality." Those who excel in leadership demonstrate the following qualities:

1. They can be counted on. In other words, they follow through on their commitments. They don't just say they are going to do something. They do it.

2. They are continually improving. They focus on being better tomorrow than they are today. They are forever on the practice field, paying careful attention to details.

3. They are greatly respected because of their character.

4. They are not just talent-focused. They are performance-focused.

5. They have a passion for what they do. In other words, they have learned how to fuel the fire that keeps them going.

3rd Key – Pay Careful Attention To Where You Have Come From and Where You Are Headed

"Know well the condition of your flocks, and pay attention to your herds" (Proverbs 27:23, *NASB*). Where are you in the process of realizing your dream? Are you paying careful attention to where you have come from and where you are heading? There are so many things that look good on the surface but are really

designed to get you off course. Here are a few action steps designed to help you keep on track:

Action Step #1 – Constantly be reminded daily of your "Why" and remind others. One of the most successful businesses I personally know has its "Why" and "What" written on a big poster board. It's the first thing you see when you enter the lobby of their offices. Any way you can visually and verbally proclaim your "Why," directly relates to the success of realizing your dreams.

Action Step #2 – Make yourself accountable to others. Share your dream with others and ask them if they would be willing to hold you accountable. Accountability accomplishes many things. First of all, it acts as a sounding board for your ideas in the process of the journey. Secondly, it acts as an encourager to accomplish certain tasks because there are people who are going to ask you how that weight loss is going, or how the book is coming along, or where you are in getting that business going? You see, it's easier to give up when no one is looking. Your accountability group inspires you to stay in the game. And thirdly, as Proverbs 27:17 tells us, *"Iron sharpens iron, and one man sharpens another"* (*ESV*). Accountability helps you sharpen your plans with the diversity of giftings and skills of those in your accountability group.

Action Step #3 – Just as I had enlisted my neighbor to be the head of my Pumpkin Guard Patrol to safeguard against pumpkin smashers, you will need to set up safeguards in realizing your dreams. There are things that you can do to protect your dream. First of all, be careful of the inner circle in which you surround yourself. Ask yourself these questions: Are they all on the same bus? In other words, are they all headed in the same direction?

Are they people of faith? Are they people who will be honest with you in a constructive manner? Secondly, you can protect your dream by *not* sharing it with everyone, because everyone doesn't have your best interest in mind. We could call those people "Dream Killers."

4th Key – Goal Setting

Bill Copeland said, "The trouble with not having a goal is that you can spend your life running up and down the field and never score." This is similar to the person who says I am *going to* write a book or start an exercise program. A year from now, three years, five years or more, they are still saying it, but it never gets done. Goal setting gives you clarity on what you ultimately want. Let's say it's your dream to build a house. You're going to need a plan. Planning makes you crystallize and articulate the desires floating in your mind. It ensures that you are channeling your time, energy, and efforts into things that really matter to you. It makes you live more consciously.

A second thing that goal setting does is that it helps you to stay on track, to stay focused on the journey of realizing your dreams. It's that laser beam focus. *"So I do not run without a goal. I fight like a boxer who is hitting something—not just the air"* (I Corinthians 9:26, *NCV*). It's really quite easy to get swept away by the currents of everyday life. The lack of goals and a plan detailing how they will be accomplished, will keep you drifting through life without realizing your dreams.

A third thing that goals do, as Ron Alford, a business coach for Southwestern Consulting says, "It helps to build character. The only thing we take to heaven is our character. Character can be summarized simply by becoming like Jesus." Philippians 3:12 describes it this way: *"I do not mean that I am already as God wants me to be. I have not yet reached that goal, but I continue trying to reach it and to make it mine. Christ wants me to do that, which is the reason He made me His"* (*NCV*).

Fourthly, as we set our goals, they need to be S.M.A.R.T. goals. Specific, Measureable, Attainable, Reviewed constantly, and on a Time frame.

Fifthly, as you set goals, be sure you do it with a plan in mind. Antoine de Saint-Exupéry said, "A goal without a plan is just a wish." My good friend, John, said this about goals: "I have struggled at times with goal accomplishment because I ignored a plan. Only now do I understand that after I identify a goal, I must develop and implement a plan to accomplish that goal."

And lastly, the main motivation behind the

setting of every goal should be love. Then we will always ask, *"How can this goal not only help me to achieve my dreams, but how will this goal also affect others?"* For instance, my dream may be to start a business. When love is the motivating factor behind my goal setting, then significance becomes the bigger picture. I come to view my business, not only as making a profit, but also as a way to share that profit in helping to make a difference in other people's lives. John Maxwell says, "When you intentionally use your influence every day to bring about a positive change in the lives of others, you achieve significance." Ron, owner of a local spice company, shares what has happened both in his life and his business when he made the main motivation of his business: **LOVE OTHERS.** "I found that as my company started giving back to God, the community and its employees, and to people in need, His generous hand became very apparent.

The truths of so many scriptures exploded into my life. How can you deny the truth of Proverbs 11:25, *"A generous person will prosper; whoever refreshes others will be refreshed" (NIV)?* This excitement of giving is contagious and transforms your and others thinking and outlook on life. Employees go with me monthly to serve homeless teenagers a great breakfast. My employees are now looking for opportunities offered by their customers to help." And Eric, the CEO of a company in Kent, Washington, had this to say: "Building a culture of love is more than just another strategy, business plan, or mission. It is the bedrock of why and how we exist. It's very exciting to see your employees exhibiting a culture of love at a charity event. They are not only engaging with the people from the charity, but they are also connecting with their fellow employees."

BELIEVE YOUR DREAM

It doesn't matter what others tell you about your dreams or the negativity that may have plagued you since childhood or the failures of your past. This can all be redirected to get you out of your rut of impossibility. Joel Osteen said, "It takes the same energy to worry as it does to believe." The first thing that will help you in believing your dream is how you handle setbacks.

Handling Setbacks

You may have tried many times and failed numerous times, but your life is not over. There is an amazing future in front of you. You are never too far-gone. Don't let anyone tell you that you will never amount to anything. Don't let your thoughts convince you that you have made so many mistakes that God would never use you. Remember the Bible story of Job and what he went through. It's as if he were standing right now in our presence saying, "I have been going through some really tough times, and I was about to give up. My wife even told me to curse God and die. I felt depressed, but I said 'Though He slay me, yet will I trust Him.' I am happy to report that God didn't just bring me out of my mess, but He brought me out better than I was before. I got my health back, I got my business back, and got my dreams back." I believe Job is saying to all who are going through tough times and have suffered loss in a family, in relationships, in finances, and in business, "I am here to tell you there is a blessing coming your way. Your circumstances may look like it's the end, but it's not. God is going to turn it around on your behalf. He's a God who specializes in new beginnings. You are going to come out stronger and healthier than ever. You may have lost your job, but don't go around complaining; instead say, 'God, I want to thank You for my new job.'" Somebody violated your trust in a relationship, walked out on you, betrayed you? Don't run around bitter, feeling sorry for yourself saying, "Poor old me." Quit wallowing around in self-pity. Get over your bitterness. Get in agreement with God and watch Him open the door for a *great* blessing in your life.

Many of us have had unfair things happen to us. We have lost our joy and are just getting by enduring life. Yet there was one who steps into the scene of life. His name is Lazarus. "I was in the grave. I was buried. It was all over. It was finished, but I had two sisters that dared to believe that with Jesus anything is possible. They rolled back the stone. Jesus spoke life. And I came back from the dead." Listen, it's not too late. It's not over. God can still bring your dream back to life. God can resurrect those dead dreams. Don't tell me you're too old, or you've made too many mistakes, or you've failed so many times. I've missed out on numerous opportunities, but the same God who brought Lazarus back to life is the same God who is about to resurrect those dreams you have already given up on. So you need to get ready. You are not limited by your circumstances, or by your past. You can rise higher. It may look impossible with men; but with God all things, I say *all* things, are possible.

Personally, I went through some trials and tribulations of my own. In 1997, I thought my life was done and all my dreams were washed up. In a period of six months, my wife of twenty-six years left me; I lost my dog; my car burned; and I went bankrupt. I virtually had no money. Everything I had hoped for—every dream gone. I know what it is to feel the pain and humiliation of financial loss. I know what it is to raise my children flawlessly and see them struggle in their walk and lifestyle. I know what it is to feel fear and rejection when you lose your job. Through all this I learned what it is to cry out, "What am I going to do?!" It was David who cried out in Psalms 61:2, *"When my heart is overwhelmed; lead me to the rock that is higher than I" (NKJV)*. When my mentor friends told me that I needed to cut the sick pumpkin from the vine, at that moment I thought I was finished, done, the journey of my dream gone.

No matter how long or dark your tunnel may appear, you are going to make it. God is at work for you. He is a God of turnarounds. He is a God of new beginnings. We can enter into His throne room—the throne room for mercy and grace. When we need more grace to get through our problems, we receive it. When we need His mercy and ask for His forgiveness because we feel condemnation and guilt, He faithfully gives it.

God is masterfully using the broken pieces of my wounded soul, taking me from ashes to beauty, restoring my life far beyond my wildest dreams and blessing me with Karilyn, my wife, and her daughter and son, giving us a blended family of six awesome God-fearing children, twenty grandchildren and one great grandchild. When we move on from our past, it liberates us into our destiny.

Joel Osteen says, "When the negative thoughts come—and they will; they come to all of us—it's not enough to just not dwell on it...you've got to replace it with a positive thought." He further says, "Every setback means you're one step closer to seeing the dream come to pass." I was thinking the other day about the dreams I have had, how I have been confronted with a lot of obstacles and fears; yet through them all, God has been faithful in teaching me to not give up. You might have a bunch more obstacles but just keep persevering. Keep believing that every setback, every failure has brought you just one step closer to the success of your dream. Believe that your dream is all about the *journey*.

Great Faith for Your Dream

Faith can mean just doing what the world may perceive as absolutely ridiculous. Many years back, when I was experiencing a major crisis in my life and about ready to lose my house to the bank, I remembered the story of Joshua and how God instructed him. Joshua 6:4—5 says, *"…on the seventh day you shall march around the city seven times, and the priests shall blow the trumpets. It shall be that when they make a long blast with the ram's horn, and when you hear the sound of the trumpet, all the people shall shout with a great shout; and the wall of the city will fall down flat, and the people will go up every man straight ahead" (NASB).* If God can bring the walls of Jericho down, certainly He can bring the walls of indifference down that were keeping my house from selling. So the very next morning in the midst of a rainstorm on Saturday, the seventh day, my son and I, along with one of his friends, began to march around our house, banging on pots and pans, praising the Lord, and thanking Him by faith for the sale of the house, with neighbors looking on thinking we had lost our minds. At the end of the seventh time around the house, we gave a huge shout of thanksgiving. Well, the very next day around noon, my daughter called me to tell me that she had run into someone at church who was interested in seeing my house. These folks came over that very afternoon and within two hours wrote a check for the entire amount of the house, including what was owed the bank in back payments, and an additional thousand dollars to me personally to find a place to rent. So, let me remind you of this truth that should fire up your faith: God is *infinitely bigger* than your biggest problem or your biggest dream.

Right Attitudes

This brings us to our third point in believing your dream. Right attitude is a necessity for the success of your dream. This is the kind of attitude that gets you up in the morning to look out the window, without regard for the weather or any surrounding circumstances, and say, "This is the day the Lord has made, I will rejoice and be glad in it!" This is the kind of attitude that sees the blossoms on the trees and hears the birds singing. It is the kind of attitude that lives the day with the expectation: "What, God, are you up to today?" This is the kind of attitude that knows no turning back whether it's one yard at a time or one inch at a time. The fulfillment and the success of your dream is a daily thing. You can be successful one day, one moment, one decision at a time. John Maxwell said, "If you can handle today correctly, tomorrow will take care of itself." This is the kind of attitude that never quits no matter what the challenge or difficulty. You may be knocked down, but you are not knocked out.

In June and July of 2012, I was hit with a situation that, in my wildest imagination, I never would have thought could happen. My 36-year-old son suffered a stroke; and thirty days later, my daughter of 38 years lay in intensive care with a ruptured aneurysm. No, I can't tell you that through all this I had perfect attitudes. I struggled with every kind of emotion you can name. I asked, "Why God?" I thought, "I'm an old man. Why couldn't it have been me instead?" No parent wants this for his or her children. And yet, I have continually been reminded of my Heavenly Father's words in Romans 8:28: *"And we know that God causes all things to work together for good to those who love God, to those who are called according to His purpose"* *(NASB).* May I remind you it is *all* things—whatever you encounter in your life, *no* exceptions. At that point I could have either focused on all the pain and emotion and on what God hadn't done yet, or I could begin to focus on His Word that "all things work to the good." So my focus changed to the little miracles that happen each day: the new words that I heard when my daughter said to me "I love you;" and when my son repeatedly said, "Dad, we're going to make it." That's right. My son did make it although my daughter, to this day, is still bedridden. I will not give up hope and neither should you. *You* are going to make it no matter what you're facing. Your dreams will be realized. Furthermore, the right attitude for the success of your dream doesn't complain or look for excuses. As George Washington Carver said, "Ninety-nine percent of the failures come from people who have the habit of making excuses."

5

PASSION FOR YOUR DREAM

In your journey of establishing your dreams, you're going to need passion for your dreams. This is what gets you up in the morning. *Passion* is defined in Merriam Webster as, "A strong feeling of enthusiasm or excitement for something or about doing something." It further says, "Intense, driving, or over-mastering feeling or conviction."

Passion is a desire that is stronger than death, stronger than any criticism, and stronger than any opposition. If you are willing to lay it all down for your dream, then you are a passionate leader. It's passion that gets you through the discouraging times. A few years back, I recall a time when I was watching my favorite college basketball team play. Much to my displeasure they were down by eleven points with only seven minutes to play in the game. When the cameras focused on one young player during a time-out, I noticed his eyes filled with passion and anticipation. The whistle blew, and they commenced the game. What happened in those next few minutes is a testimony of what passion will do. This young man's passion ignited the whole team. As the crowd cheered in those few remaining minutes, the game completely turned around. We won by fourteen points! One man's passion for those few moments changed the course of that game. Your passion for your dream will ignite those around you. Passion is contagious. With passion, we set an atmosphere for success. It was John Wooden, the former UCLA

Basketball coach, who said, "It's not so important who starts the game but who finishes it." Passion is that desire that doesn't quit no matter what the circumstances. If it gets tough, you just get tougher.

The apostle Paul accomplished an astounding amount in two decades of ministry. What made him tick? What drove him to carry out the work that he did? We find the secret in Philippians 3:7—9: *"The very credentials these people are waving around as something special, I'm tearing up and throwing out with the trash—along with everything else I used to take credit for. And why? Because of Christ. Yes, all the things I once thought were so important are gone from my life. Compared to the high privilege of knowing Christ Jesus as my Master, firsthand, everything I once thought I had going for me is insignificant—dog dung. I've dumped it all in the trash so that I could embrace Christ and be embraced by Him. I didn't want some petty, inferior brand of righteousness that comes from keeping a list of rules when I could get the robust kind that comes from trusting Christ—God's righteousness" (The Message).* That passage explodes with Paul's passion for his calling. Effective leaders, like Paul, are those who have figured out what they stand for. They have identified their purpose and pursue it with a passion. As you may recall, it was passion and anticipation for growing my pumpkin that brought great excitement every morning and every evening.

I think of my maternal grandfather Larson who was an immigrant from Sweden. His dream was to come to America and buy a farm in the state of northern Idaho. His journey to his dream began with his traveling from Sweden to the Alaska Gold Rush, where he was able to be one of the fortunate ones to strike gold. From there, his journey took him to Black Diamond, Washington. It was there where he sent for my grandmother to come from

Sweden. She was what they called a *mail-order bride*. It was there where my mother was born, and my grandpa would continue to work in the coal mine. All this time, with his focus and his determination for his dream, he continued to save his money. When he had enough, he helped to pack up the family and move to a little town in Northern Idaho called Leland. There he bought a farm. He had a dream. He believed the dream one step at a time.

How is your journey going? Are you still on the journey, or have you dropped out? It's time to change your attitude. Stop letting your past setbacks and failures dictate your present and future. It's never too late to dream again. Remember, God gave you that dream in the first place. Stop wasting what God placed in your heart. It's not too late; come on, make a decision. Start today. DREAM BIG!

6

THE SIGNIFICANCE OF YOUR DREAM

"For even the Son of Man did not come to be served, but to serve, and to give His life a ransom for many" (Mark 10:45, *NASB*). To really live our dream, we must give up on self-centeredness and self-fulfillment and realize that the success of our dreams is something much bigger—something outside of our self. It's making a difference in others. John Maxwell said this about significance: "Do you know the difference between success and significance? I know a lot of people who believe they are successful because they have everything they want. They have added value to

themselves. But I believe significance comes when you add value to others—and you can't have true success without significance." Your dream may be to start a business or to write a book or even to start an exercise program. The real success of any dream can be measured by how effective it is in making a difference and bringing value into someone else's life. For instance, if you will recall in my story, it was my dream to grow the biggest pumpkin. With that in mind, I had to establish my "Why." It would obviously be self-fulfilling and self-focused if my "Why" was simply to win bragging rights and to be declared the greatest pumpkin grower. But on the other hand, having the opportunity to teach my neighbor to grow pumpkins and grow them together the next year would mean I was seeing my pumpkin growing as something much larger than myself. And to enlarge the picture even further, Heather, CEO of a company in Bellevue, Washington, challenged me to share my pumpkin with others by baking pumpkin bread. She even gave me the recipe! With the help of my wife, Karilyn, my mission was accomplished. My dream was shared with nearly one hundred people. What are your dreams and how do you measure their success?

A DIALOGUE ON PARTING THOUGHTS

This dialogue guide is broken down into six sessions for your discussion. Discuss each thought by dealing with each question. From this dialogue, begin to create some action steps that you can take to realize your dreams. Remember that the best dialogue takes place when people feel the freedom to share their thoughts. Pray before each dialogue session, specifically asking the Holy Spirit to lead and give wisdom to your discussion.

Session 1: Chapter 1

The realization of your dreams really starts with a seed, much like an idea or a thought. How many innovative and creative ideas have you had in the course of your life only to find yourself saying, "I should have done something with that idea?"

1. What are some of the ideas you have had?

2. What things have kept you from pursuing your dreams?

3. What are you doing about it?

I was so excited and full of anticipation that when I arrived home from work, I would walk over to my pumpkin pot and poke my finger into the soil where I had planted the seed.

1. What does it mean to have anticipation for your dream?

2. What moments of anticipation have you had in realizing your dreams?

Session 2: Chapter 2

In the process of beginning my journey to fulfilling my dream, I had to ask myself the hard questions about growing my pumpkin. Why am I growing this pumpkin, and what do I hope to achieve by it??

1. What is so important about establishing your "Why?"

2. What are the three reasons why the Jesus "Why" is so important in establishing your dream, and what are your thoughts about these reasons?

3. What do you think when your "What" and your "Why" go beyond yourself?

69

Sessions 3 & 4: Chapter 3

The success of your dreams is really dependent on how well you prepare. Russell Wilson, Seattle Seahawks quarterback said, "The separation is in the preparation." So often when we find that it will take a lot of effort or it will be costly and uncomfortable to complete, we shelve and just dismiss the idea.

1. Why is preparation so important?

2. In the past, what has kept you from taking the necessary steps to prepare?

3. What are some preparatory action steps you can take to breathe life into your dreams?

4. When will you start and who will hold you accountable with your progress?

Just as I needed mentorship for the success of growing my pumpkin, you need mentors with your dream.

1. Give one example of how mentorship has helped you.

2. What are the characteristics you look for in choosing mentors?

3. How many mentors do you currently have? Is that enough?

Your part in realizing your dream is to use the skills and talents that you have been given, paying attention to details, getting proper training, acquiring mentorship, and working hard.

1. How well do you believe you are utilizing your gifts and skills?

2. Are there any specific things you can do to be more effective in your skills?

3. Who are some nationally known speakers and writers that inspire and challenge you?

Where are you in your journey to realizing your

dreams? It is important to pay careful attention to where you have come and where you are headed. There are so many things that look good on the surface but are really designed to get you off track.

1. What are those rabbit trails? Can you see a common tendency?

2. List some action steps to help keep you on track.

It has been said that setting goals gives you clarity about what you ultimately want to accomplish. It helps you to crystallize and articulate the desires floating in your mind. It helps to ensure that you are channeling your time, energy, and effort into the things that really matter.

1. What is your definition of a goal?

2. What goals have you set in order to accomplish your dreams?

3. What has been your greatest dream realized so far?

Session 5: Chapters 4 & 5

It doesn't matter what others tell you about your dreams, or the negativity that you may have been plagued with, or the failures of your past. This can all be redirected to get you out of your rut. Joel Osteen said, "It takes the same energy to worry as it does to believe." Remember, God is infinitely bigger than your biggest challenge or your biggest dream.

1. How big is your perception of God?

2. When was there a time in your life you really needed the assurance that God was bigger than your mountain? Tell your story.

3. Why is negativity so damaging?

4. What steps are you willing to take to help reduce the negativity in your life?

5. What are some faith steps you can take to point you in a productive direction?

In your journey of believing for your dream you will need passion for your dream. Webster defines passion as an "intense, driving, or over-mastering feeling or conviction." *Passion* is a desire that is stronger than death, stronger than any criticism and stronger than any opposition. If you are willing to lay it all down on the line, then you are a passionate leader.

Agree or disagree? Why?

Session 6: Chapter 6

John Maxwell says, "Do you know the difference between success and significance? I know a lot of people who believe they are successful because they have everything they want. They have added value to themselves. But I believe significance comes when you add value to others—and you can't have true success without significance."

1. How do you define significance?

2. How significant-centered are your dreams?

3. What kind(s) of value have you added to others in the past?

4. Who are some people you've influenced and/ or want to influence with your dreams?

DON'T WAIT! GO NOW!

PLANT YOUR SEED!

Made in the USA
San Bernardino, CA
20 April 2018